StoryTeller
Jean Craighead George
WorkBook
Expert Writer

For more information about our company and our books, write to Lunchbox Lessons at:

970 W Broadway Suite E406, Jackson, Wyoming 83001

or visit our website

www.lunchboxlessons.com

ISBN Number: 978-1-60507-027-8

Documentary film

Storyteller: Jean Craighead George

to accompany this WorkBook available at

your local bookstore

ISBN: 978-1-60507-010-0

BrainSnack downloads available from:

Apple iTunes

Apple Learning Interchange

LunchboxLessons.com

Printed in the United States of America

Copyright 2008 by Lunchbox Lessons

Lunchbox Lessons LLC

Jackson Hole, WY 83001

Continue your adventures with these other StoryTeller WorkBooks

Jean Craighead George Titles
Beginner Writer
Intermediate Writer
Advanced Writer
Expert Writer

Ken Thomasma Titles
Story Explorer
Story Reporter
Story Giver

T.A. Barron Titles
World of Nature
World of Magic
World of Fantasy
World of Heroes

Workbook Overview

Welcome to the exciting and personalized learning experience that is yours as part of the *StoryTeller: Jean Craighead George* series. If you enjoy good books and would like to learn from one of our most beloved authors, Jean Craighead George, you've come to the right place! Using the free downloadable BrainSnacks and the activities that follow, you're in for a real treat.

Each one- to five minute BrainSnack features Jean sharing personal stories and advice about how she writes. You can view them on your iPod or your computer. After you've watched a BrainSnack as many times as you'd like, look for the activity pages in this WorkBook that go along with it.

Most of us need a prod to get ideas swirling in our heads.

Once that happens it is easy to write.

- Jean Craighead George

Lunchbox Lessons LLC

Dear Parent,

If you could choose anyone to help your child gain skills and confidence as she explores her writing talents, whom would you pick? Surely a highly acclaimed author with over 40 years of experience writing for young readers and with more than 100 books to her credit would be at the top of your list. Meet Jean Craighead George, the ideal mentor for you child.

You hold in your hands the *Expert Writers WorkBook* for the Jean Craighead Storyteller series. Throughout the WorkBook, Ms. Craighead shares her knowledge and experience to guide you and your child through creative, engaging and challenging media-based activities. Download the free one to five minute BrainSnacks onto your iPod or computer and hear Jean's personal stories and advice on writing. Each BrainSnack has coinciding activities within the WorkBook.

These appealing activities build self-confidence and skills while encouraging interaction between you and your child. Many activities involve your working with your child, helping her think of ideas before writing them down. The activities also provide your child with the chance to work independently, allowing her to grow on her own. Your main job is to be a writing coach—to help make the activities interesting and enjoyable. So join in and work with your child side-by-side! Become a writing team and have fun together. At the end of the writing journey, your child will discover that she has created her own original masterpiece and is ready to share it with the world!

Yes, your writer is ready; author Jean Craighead George is set; the creative staff at Lunchbox Lessons is waiting to help you on your way. Now all we need is YOU!

Sincerely,

Lunchbox Lessons
Your partners in progressive education

Lunchbox
Lessons
LLC

Dear Writer,

If you enjoy good books and would like to learn from one of our most beloved authors, Jean Craighead George, you've come to the right place! With Lunchbox Lessons' free downloadable BrainSnacks and the activities that follow, you're in for a real treat!

BrainSnacks are one- to five minute videos featuring Jean as she talks about how she writes. They include personal stories and sound advice that you can view on your iPod or computer as many times as you'd like. After you're done watching, look through this workbook for the activity pages that match each BrainSnack.

These activities are fun and exciting, not some boring fill-in-the-blank workbook. You'll get to go outside, explore and play games with your parents, and once you've finished this workbook you'll have created your very own story.

Now all you have to do is meet your guide, Jean. Here's what she has to say.

I write for children.
Children are still in love with the wonders of nature, and I am, too.
So I tell them stories about a boy and a falcon,
a girl and an elegant wolf pack,
about owls, weasels, foxes, prairie dogs,
the alpine tundra, the tropical rain forest.
And when the telling is done,
I hope they will want to protect all the beautiful creatures and places.

- Jean Craighead George

So dig in, meet Jean and have some fun! We know that you'll end up writing a story that you won't forget!

Sincerely,

Lunchbox Lessons
Your partners in progressive education

Lunchbox Lessons LLC

StoryTeller: Jean Craighead George
Expert Writer

Lunchbox Lessons
LLC

The software programs listed below may be referenced in the following pages, and skill level for each is noted. Tutorials for all noted software available at http://www.apple.com/support/software/

Numbers, Pages, and Keynote are available in the iWork Software Suite.

Numbers (Easy to Intermediate)
An innovative spreadsheet application that lets you organize your data to fit the way you think. Do everything from setting up the family budget to completing a lab report to creating complex financial documents.

Pages (Easy)
Writing comes naturally when you're using Pages. Start with one of over 140 templates to write beautiful letters, resumes, reports, business forms, and more. And create media-rich newsletters, brochures, and flyers with point-and-click ease.

Keynote (Easy)
Create stunning, cinema-quality presentations more easily than ever with Keynote. Use animation tools to move and scale images along a path. Or rotate them on the face of a cube or on a turntable. Add dazzling text effects and slide transitions. Even record and deliver narrated presentations.

iPhoto, iMovie, GarageBand, iWeb, and iDVD are available in the iLife Software Suite.

iPhoto (Easy)
Organize. Enhance. Share. Turn pictures into a photo book, calendar, and personal MobileMe Gallery.

iMovie (Easy)
Easily create amazing movies and share them with the world.

GarageBand (Easy)
Create and record music, make podcasts, and play with your own virtual band.

iWeb (Easy)
Quickly create a stunning website, complete with photos, movies, and live web widgets.

iDVD (Easy to Intermediate)
Turn your home movies and slideshows into gorgeous Hollywood-style DVDs.

The following software applications are sold individually for more advanced video and photography users.

Final Cut Express (Intermediate)
Edit video like a pro with Final Cut Express. Start by capturing DV, HDV and AVCHD footage or import your movie from iMovie — and discover the advanced moviemaking power at your disposal in the Open Format Timeline. Add dynamic titles and graphics using LiveType. Final Cut Express delivers all the tools you need to make great movies.

Final Cut Studio (Advanced)
Final Cut Studio is the professional award-winning video and audio production suite. With six powerful applications, each designed specifically for editors, Final Cut Studio puts everything you need in a single box: Final Cut Pro for video and film editing, Motion for graphics and animation in 3D, Soundtrack Pro for professional audio post-production, Color for professional color grading and finishing, Compressor 3 and DVD Studio Pro for digital delivery virtually anywhere — a disc, the web, Apple TV, iPod, or cell phone.

Aperture (Intermediate to Advanced)
Aperture gives photographers incredible tools to manage massive libraries, speed through photo edits, make essential image adjustments, and deliver photos online and in print using one simple, integrated workflow. Whether you shoot RAW or JPEG, Aperture lets you get the most out of your photography.

BrainSnacks - Descriptions and Downloading

BrainSnack: *Components of a Story*
"Stories are everywhere," says Storyteller Jean Craighead George, and in this BrainSnack she'll helps you weave components like plot, characters and setting into a story.

BrainSnack*: Research*
Conducting research doesn't mean spending hours in the library or on the Internet reading about a subject. As Storyteller Jean Craighead George tells us in this BrainSnack, research can be exploratory, adventurous, inspirational, eye-opening and even fun.

BrainSnack: *Create Your Story*
Stories have three elements — a beginning, middle and end — but do you always have to start at the beginning? Storyteller Jean Craighead George answers this important question.

BrainSnack: *Write about What You Know*
Are you at a loss for words? Storyteller Jean Craighead George shares her trick to letting the story write itself in this BrainSnack.

BrainSnack: *Ways to Tell a Story*
How many ways can you tell a story? In this BrainSnack, Jean Craighead George reveals several techniques a budding storyteller can use, from oral tradition and music to journalism and pictures.

Downloading

To download and view BrainSnacks for this WorkBook, visit iTunes and search under Podcasts or visit the Apple Learning Interchange at:

> http://edcommunity.apple.com/lunchboxlessons

Once there, follow the 'Lunchbox Lessons: BrainSnacks' link on the right side of the screen and then click on 'View All Items'.

Lunchbox
Lessons
LLC

Activity 1: *Meet Your Mentor*

Media Connection

Visit www.jeancraigheadgeorge.com to access biographical, bibliographical and professional background information about author Jean Craighead George.

Activity Map

1. **What is a mentor?** Throughout this WorkBook, you'll be working with author Jean Craighead George, who will serve as your writing mentor. A mentor is a knowledgeable, respected and trusted guide and advisor. Using a thesaurus, find synonyms (words which have the same or nearly the same meaning) for mentor and write them below.

_____

_____

2. **Who is Jean Craighead George?** Go to Jean Craighead George's website (www.jeancraigheadgeorge.com) and search for answers to this question. Write down what you find on the lines below.

_____

_____

_____

_____

3. **What have you read?** Jean has written over 100 books for young people. Look at the partial list below and mark the appropriate columns for books you've read or heard of and books that you are interested in reading.

Read or heard of	Interested in reading	Book title
		Arctic Son
		The Case of the Missing Cutthroats: An Ecological Mystery
		Cliff Hanger
		The Cry of the Crow
		Dipper of Copper Creek
		Fire Storm
		The First Thanksgiving
		Julie
		Julie of the Wolves
		Julie's Wolf Pack
		Look to the North, A Wolf Pup Diary
		Luck, The Story of a Sandhill Crane
		My Side of the Mountain
		Nutik and Amaroq Play Ball
		On the Far Side of the Mountain
		One Day in the Alpine Tundra
		One Day in the Desert
		One Day in the Prairie
		One Day in the Tropical Rain Forest
		The Summer of the Falcon
		The Talking Earth
		The Thirteen Moons series
		There's an Owl in the Shower
		Who Really Killed Cock Robin: An Ecological Mystery
		The Wolves are Back

4. **Find that book!** Visit your local library or bookstore to find one of the books you would like to read, and begin! Reading as many works by a given author as you can will help you better understand that author's writing style and thematic focus.

Activity Extension

Jean once said that she and her family would often tell stories around the dinner table when she was young. Take time to share with your family what you've learned about the author and the books she has written.

Activity 2: *Protagonists and Settings*

Media Connection

Visit www.jeancraigheadgeorge.com and browse the Writing link.

Activity Map

1. **Who's who in a story?** A protagonist is the main character in a work of fiction. There will always be an endless supply of possible protagonists for any story you write. Think of three books or stories you have read and list a protagonist from each. Include a description of what that character was like. If you know the title of the book or story, list it as well.

_____

_____

_____

2. **Can you describe a protagonist's role?** Choose one of the protagonists you listed. Use the lines below to describe what this character's role in the story was. Describe what this character did, whether they changed from the beginning to the end of the story and how they interacted with other characters.

_____

_____

_____

_____

3. **Name those characters!** Choose several possible protagonists for your story and list them on the lines below. Give each a name or a short descriptive identifier, but don't develop them completely just yet.

Potential protagonist #1: _____

_____

Potential protagonist #2: _____

_____

Potential protagonist #3: _____

_____

4. **Where will it be?** A story's setting is the time and location where a story occurs. Where and when would you like your story to take place? Is it somewhere you could realistically visit? Jean Craighead George often recommends choosing a location you know well so you can describe it realistically. Make a list of several possible story locations. Be as specific as you can.

Possible story location #1: _____

Possible story location #2: _____

Possible story location #3: _____

5. **Pick a setting.** Choose the location you like best. Keep in mind that a location you can physically visit would be best for this activity.

My story location choice: _____

6. **On with the show!** If the location of your story is a place you will need to visit via car, discuss the travel plans with your parent. Use the travel planner below to organize the visit. If an actual visit is not possible, decide how you will learn as much as possible about the site you wish to write about without physically observing the place.

When will you visit? _____

How will you get there? _____

Who will go with you? _____

What writing supplies might you need? _____

7. **When can I start?** Before going to your story location, advance to the next activity!

Activity Extension
Return to a few of your favorite books from childhood, ones you haven't read for a while. Reacquaint yourself with the protagonists in these stories. Ask yourself why the characters are memorable.

Activity 3: *Searching for Story Ideas*

Media Connection

Download BrainSnack: *Components of a Story* and have an iPod or computer ready to watch it on. You can find instructions on downloading BrainSnacks at the beginning of your WorkBook.

Ask your parent to take you to your chosen story location.

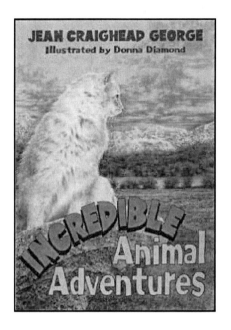

Activity Map

1. **What did she say?** View BrainSnack: *Components of a Story* a second time. Early in the BrainSnack, Jean Craighead George describes what it is she does when she is looking around for story ideas. Use the lines below to write what she says.

_____

_____

_____

_____

_____

_____

2. **How do you find those story ideas?** Visit the location you described in the previous activity as the setting you have chosen for your story. When you are on the spot, make note of the following details.

List the location's sights here.

_____

_____

_____

_____

List the location's sounds here.

_____

_____

_____

_____

List the location's smells here.

_____

_____

_____

_____

Can you make any other observations? List them here.

_____

_____

_____

_____

Can you think of any story ideas that could take place in this spot? List them here.

_____

_____

_____

_____

_____

_____

_____

Activity Extension

Take an audio or video recorder with you as you visit your story location. Record sights and sounds which are difficult to capture in words. Keep the recordings handy for reference as your story develops.

Activity 4: *Delving into More Research*

Media Connection

Download BrainSnack: *Research* and have an iPod or computer ready to   watch it on. You can find instructions on downloading BrainSnacks at the beginning of your WorkBook.

Activity Map

1. **Are we there yet?** Yes, you are almost ready to begin writing. Jean Craighead George suggests fastening pictures in your mind of your story's location in order to make the writing experience more rich and enjoyable.

2. **BrainSnack time!** View BrainSnack: *Research*. While you're watching, complete Jean's statements

"You have to put yourself _____

"I paint when I go_____

"To draw pictures just _____

3. **Time to go back.** Your location is calling you! Return with writing materials and art supplies in hand. Follow the advice of Jean Craighead George by doing one or more of the following.
   - Paint when you go on these field trips to keep the place alive and fresh in your mind for future reference.
   - Put yourself into the heads of the creatures there by writing about what you imagine could happen in the place.
   - Draw pictures to fasten images in your mind when you are back home, creating your storylines and developing your characters.
   - Use the next two pages for this activity.

4. **Return to your writing desk.** Use the field notes, sketches and paintings you completed to prepare yourself for the actual writing of your story. In BrainSnack: *Research*, Jean Craighead George states that having "all of this information packed into my head makes writing easier."

5. **Delving deeper.** Search the Internet for more details about your setting. For example, there might be historical information that could surface in your story or play a critical role in the plot. Make notes or attach additional information below.

Activity Extension

Bring your protagonist to life. In the space below, sketch a picture of one of your characters in the location you have described, drawn, or painted. What actions do you see your protagonist doing there? Remember, action leads to plot, and plot leads to the next activity!

Activity 5: *We've Got Problems!*

Media Connection

Download BrainSnack: *Research* and have an iPod or computer ready to watch it on. You can find instructions on downloading BrainSnacks at the beginning of your WorkBook.

> **PARENT TIP**
>
> AS YOUR CHILD BEGINS IMAGINING CONFLICTS AND PROBLEMS FOR HER CHARACTERS, BE AVAILABLE TO SHARE YOUR EXPERIENCES WITH CONFLICTS AND PROBLEMS IF YOUR CHILD NEEDS HELP. BE CAREFUL TO ONLY PROVIDE SUGGESTIONS WHEN YOUR CHILD ASKS FOR THEM.

Activity Map

1. **Take advice from Jean Craighead George!** In the BrainSnacks you have viewed, Jean talks about problems that make life and stories more interesting. As you begin the creation and development of the plot of your story, remember to give your protagonist a problem to solve or a conflict to resolve. Write some ideas down on the lines below.

_____

_____

_____

_____

_____

_____

_____

2. **Think about your own experiences!** In these BrainSnacks, Jean Craighead George also suggests that writers should write about experiences they have had. She says, "Think about your own problems. Use one of your own worries. You will write better if you do." Without stating too much detail, list two or three of your own problems on the next page.

Problem #1: _____

Problem #2: _____

Problem #3: _____

3. **What problems will the protagonists in your story face?** Think of a problem your main character might face as your story unfolds. Now, use that problem to fill out the lines below.

Protagonist _____

List problem _____

Describe the problem in some detail _____

_____

_____

_____

4. **Who are the other characters?** Usually there is more than just one character in a story. Think about all the possible people your protagonist might come to know as your story unfolds. Will these characters be friends or foes or just bystanders? Briefly list your character ideas here.

Character 1:_____

_____

_____

Character 2:_____

_____

_____

Character 3:_____

_____

_____

Character 4:_____

_____

_____

Activity Extension

Spend a few hours, or even a whole day, imagining you are a character in your story. Act and talk the way your character would. Feel how it is to be the character you have created! Remember the advice Jean Craighead George has given you; "Put yourself into the heads of the creatures [or people] you are writing about."

Activity 6: *From the Beginning*

Media Connection

Download BrainSnack: *Create Your Story* and have an iPod or computer ready to watch it on. You can find instructions on downloading BrainSnacks at the beginning of your WorkBook.

Activity Map

1. **BrainSnack time!** View BrainSnack: *Create Your Story*. Afterward, use the lines below to summarize what Jean Craighead George says about the beginning, middle and end of a story.

_____

_____

_____

_____

_____

_____

_____

> **PARENT TIP**
>
> THIS IS A GOOD TIME TO ENCOURAGE YOUR CHILD'S WRITING. IF SHE ASKS FOR HELP, READ HER WORK AND GIVE CONSTRUCTIVE FEEDBACK ABOUT THE STORYLINE AND CHARACTER DEVELOPMENT. DON'T WORRY ABOUT SPELLING AND GRAMMAR YET.
>
> YOU CAN ALSO PROVIDE YOUR CHILD WITH SOME THINK TIME SNACKS.

2. **Ready … Set … Go! Your story is about to unfold!** Review all of the WorkBook activities you've completed so far in order to refresh yourself on your setting and characters. Then, begin writing your story using your the spaces below and on the next few pages. While writing, keep these tips in mind.

   • Try to visualize the story in your mind.

   • Choose your point of view. Are you going to write in the first person, pretending that you are in the story and writing with the pronoun "I", or in the third person, pretending that you're watching the story and writing with the pronouns "he" or "she"?

   • Heed Jean's advice about story beginnings — "The beginning is always hard, so … put it down and then go on; otherwise you'll stop forever on the beginning. Just move on and then go back."

_____

_____

_____

_____

_____

_____

_____

_____

_____

_____

Lunchbox Lessons LLC

Activity Extension

Give yourself a break! Authors need plenty of THINK TIME during the writing process. Don't feel guilty about times when your pencil is not moving. It's important to stop periodically and take a walk, have a snack or do something that has nothing to do with your writing. When you come back you will feel refreshed and ready to move forward.

Activity 7: *The Meaty Middle*

Media Connection

Download BrainSnack: *Write about What You Know* and have an iPod or computer ready to watch it on. You can find instructions on downloading BrainSnacks at the beginning of your WorkBook.

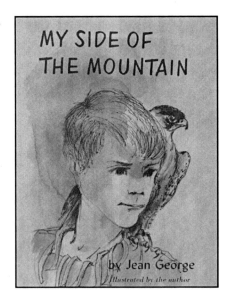

Activity Map

1. **Add that ambiance.** Jean Craighead George suggests that "the middle of the story should cover the action and the ambiance." Look up the word ambiance and define it in your own words on the lines below.

_____

_____

2. **Write a sentence** that describes the ambiance of your story's setting. Try to write two sentences, one that uses the word ambiance and one that doesn't.

_____

_____

_____

_____

3. **Spice it up.** Jean Craighead George also says that, "The middle of a story brings in other people or animals to enhance the plot." Below, list two or three characters you have chosen to introduce in the middle of your story.

Character 1: _____

Character 2: _____

Character 3: _____

4. **BrainSnack!** Watch BrainSnack: *Write about What You Know.* Then, ask yourself if you know your characters and location well enough to be able to write about them easily. If not, go back and do some more research on them. Once you feel that you know them well enough, choose two or three of the characters or places in your story. List them below and write everything you know about them.

Character/Place #1:_____

What I Know:_____

_____

_____

Character/Place #2:_____

What I Know:_____

_____

_____

Character/Place #3:_____

What I know: _____

_____

_____

5. Add the action and advance. The middle is the meaty part of the story. Continue writing your story, connecting your beginning with the middle and adding characters, conflict and suspense! Use the spaces below and on the next three pages.

_____

_____

_____

_____

_____

_____

_____

_____

_____

_____

_____

_____

Lunchbox
Lessons
LLC

_____

_____

_____

_____

_____

_____

_____

_____

_____

_____

_____

_____

_____

_____

_____

_____

_____

Lunchbox
Lessons
LLC

Activity Extension

If your story turns out to be larger than you first imagined, you might want to turn it into an entire book. Grab your parent or a friend and share your ideas while planning out the plot. Remember, J.K. Rowling, the author of the *Harry Potter* series, has said in many interviews that she outlined the entire plot of the *Harry Potter* books before she had even written the first one!

Lunchbox
Lessons
LLC

Activity 8: *Exciting Ending*

Media Connection

Download BrainSnack: *Ways to Tell a Story* and have an iPod or computer ready to watch it on. You can find instructions on downloading BrainSnacks at the beginning of your WorkBook.

> **PARENT TIP**
>
> NOW IS A GOOD TIME TO HELP YOUR CHILD STAY ON TASK AND NOT WALK AWAY AND FORGET ABOUT THEIR STORY. BE SURE NOT TO NAG OR BADGER HER, THOUGH; YOU WANT TO MAKE SURE SHE'S STILL HAVING FUN.

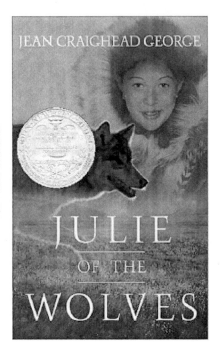

JEAN CRAIGHEAD GEORGE

JULIE
OF THE
WOLVES

Activity Map

1. **The beginning of the end.** Jean Craighead George claims that story endings are the most fun! Use the lines below to explain why you think she would say that.

    _____

    _____

2. **Jean also says**, "Suddenly, your character, in its setting, will take over and do things you never thought about before you started writing." Have you found your character or setting taking over as you write? If so, describe that time on the lines below.

    _____

    _____

    _____

3. **BrainSnack time!** Watch BrainSnack: *Ways to Tell a Story.* Summarize what Jean Craighead George has to say about what it is you have to have in order to be a writer.

_____

_____

_____

_____

4. **Beginning the end.** Jean Craighead George has suggested that your story's ending will write itself, but don't forget that she has also talked about discipline. Ideas may come swiftly as your story nears its end, but you are the only one who can tie all the loose ends together. Write the end of your story using the lines below and on the next two pages.

_____

_____

_____

_____

_____

_____

_____

Activity Extension

You may be able to get a jump start on your story polishing. Find a quiet place and read your story out loud. Many times gaps in the story, unnecessary repetition or misuse of words will become apparent when you read your writing out loud.

Activity 9: *Read and Revise*

Media Connection

Review all of the BrainSnacks (*Components of a Story, Research, Create Your Story, Write About What You Know* and *Ways to Tell a Story*) that you watched in this WorkBook. Review the Writing page on Jean Craighead George's website.

Activity Map

These writing activities are like the last inning, the closing seconds and the final hit of the big game. You need to give your writing all the attention it deserves in order to finish it successfully. So adjust your helmet, tighten your shoes, step up to the plate and get ready for the last sprint around the bases!

1. **Time out and away.** If you have made it this far, you are a dedicated writer. Before proceeding to revising and editing, however, you need to take a break. This break will refresh you before you move on to the next phase, the editing process. Your break might be a few hours, a day or a whole week. Write down the length of your break and its location.

Length of break:_____

Location of break:_____

2. **Read and revise.** Welcome back! Once you're done with your break, use the checklist below as you work through the revision process.

    —— Read your story aloud to yourself. Look at each word and sentence and ask yourself:

    ◦ Is there a way to make a description of a place, person or event more clear?

    ◦ Are my word choices too simple or too complex?

    —— Use words that your audience will understand. Make changes as needed.

—— Look for places where you *tell* instead of *show*. *Showing* lets readers *see* the action. *Telling* simply states the action and does not require readers to use their imagination. Try to think of ways to change *telling* sentences to *showing* sentences.

—— Find a thesaurus and replace overused and dull words with more graphic ones. If you don't know how to use a thesaurus, ask a parent or teacher.

—— Read your writing out loud to a parent or to another adult. Pause after each paragraph or page and ask for suggestions. Make notes on your hard copy with a colored pencil or pen.

Activity Extension

You might want to add illustrations to your story at this point. You could make full page drawings to insert between pages or sketches of characters and events to insert before section headings. Use the next two pages to illustrate your story.

Lunchbox
Lessons
LLC

Activity 10: *The Final Proof!*

Media Connection

Review all of the BrainSnacks (*Components of a Story, Research, Create Your Story, Write About What You Know* and *Ways to Tell a Story*) that you watched in this WorkBook.

JEAN CRAIGHEAD GEORGE
Shark Beneath the Reef

Activity Map

1. **Editors look at the little things.** It's time to look at the little things that will make a big difference in your finished product. Follow the checklist below as you go through the editing process.

   —— Run a spell check.

   —— Look for diction errors (words used incorrectly). Some common errors are listed below.

   ◦ Loose/Lose
   Loose is an adjective — "a *loose* wire."
   Lose is a verb — "we will *lose* the race."

   ◦ Its/It's
   Its is a possessive form of *it*, similar to the possessive pronouns his or hers — "The house has a roof. *Its* chimney is broken."
   It's is a contraction of *it is* — "*It's* not always easy to keep the two straight."

   ◦ Lay/Lie
   Lay is a verb which is followed by a direct object — "A hen *lays* an egg."
   Lie is a verb which is not followed by a direct object — "The dog *lies* in the corner."
   The confusion *lies* with the use of the past tense of *lie* which is *lay* — "The dog *lay* in the corner all day yesterday."

   ◦ To/Too
   To is used as a preposition or with an infinitive — "It is time *to* go *to* school."

Too is another word for *also* — "Can I come, *too?*"
Too is also used as an adverbial intensifier — "You are *too* beautiful for words."

○ Than/Then
Than is a conjunction which indicates a comparison — "Mike is larger *than* Fred."
Then is an adverb of time indicating a sequence of events — "I traveled to Mars and *then* on to the moon."

○ I/Me
I is the subject pronoun — "That dog is larger than *I* (am)."
Me is the object pronoun — "The teacher explained the story to Harry, Maria, Leo and *me.*"

—— Check for errors in punctuation usage. Some examples are listed below.

○ Apostrophes
"That is *Henry's* house." "The *horses'* stables were cleaned."

○ Quotation marks
"We are ready," said the coach. "Let's start the game!"

○ Commas
in a series — "Ted walked, jogged and then sprinted to school."
with compound sentences — "Ron likes reading the newspaper, but I like reading magazines."
to set off appositives — "Roberta, the queen of the fair, wore her crown to bed."

○ Semi-colons join compound sentences without a conjunction
"Ron likes reading the newspaper; I like reading magazines."

—— Look for grammatical errors like the ones below.

○ Incomplete sentences
"Ron reading the newspaper." (wrong)
"Ron was reading the newspaper." (right)

○ Run-on sentence
"Ron walked I jogged and Roberta crawled to the swing set." (wrong)
"Ron walked, I jogged and Roberta crawled." (right)

○ Misplaced modifiers

"It was easy to see the ballgame sitting in the bleachers." (wrong)
"Sitting in the bleachers, we could easily see the ball game." (right)

- Parallelism (forms that do not match)
"Rita likes swimming, jogging and to dance." (wrong)
"Rita likes to swimming, jogging and dancing." (right)

- Verb and noun agreement
"Each girl really liked their book." (wrong)
"Each girl really liked her book." (right)

- Inconsistent verb tenses
"The bear cub turns toward its mom while she washed its face." (wrong)
"The bear cub turned toward its mom while she washed its face." (right)

- Use of passive voice
"Some fresh flowers were bought by Meg's mom for the party." (wrong)
"Meg's mom bought some fresh flowers for the party." (right)

—— Check for language clarity and style, being sure to avoid:
- flowery prose (too many adjectives or mixed metaphors)
- sentences that don't make sense or ideas that are off track
- characters or plot details which are not well developed.

—— Read your work aloud again, listening for variety in your sentence structure. More sophisticated writing should include sentences and paragraphs that begin in a number of different ways:
- with a subject — "The boy looked through the window."
- with a prepositional phrase — "In the middle of the night, the boy looked through the window."
- with an adverb or adverbial clause — "Slowly the boy pulled back the curtain and looked through the window."
- with a present or past participle phrase — "Looking through the window, the boy shouted in alarm!"
- with a question — "Why did the boy look through the window?"
- with an infinitive phrase — "To look through a window in the dead of night is not a good idea!"
- with an appositive — "The boy, the most curious person in the house, looked out the window."

2. **Revise again.** After editing your work, write the second-to-last draft of your story on the next seven pages.

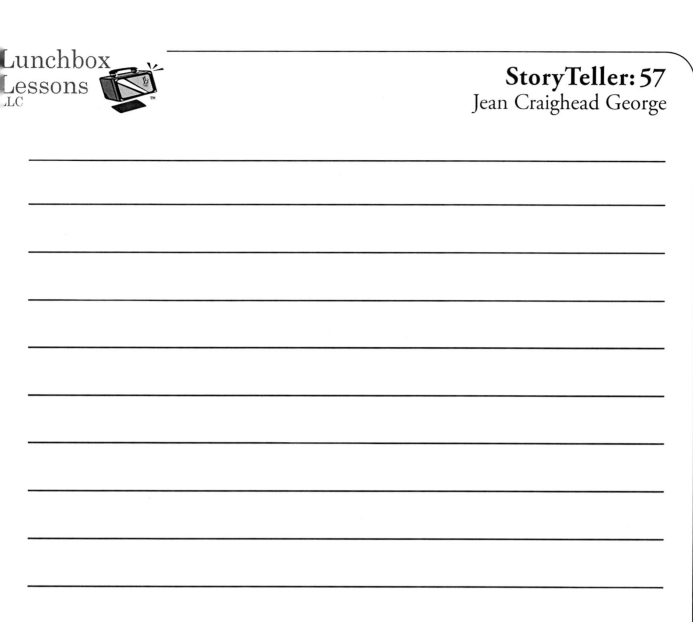

_____

_____

_____

_____

_____

_____

_____

_____

_____

_____

_____

_____

_____

_____

_____

_____

Lunchbox
Lessons
LLC

_____

_____

_____

_____

_____

_____

_____

_____

_____

_____

_____

_____

_____

_____

Lunchbox Lessons LLC

StoryTeller: 63
Jean Craighead George

3. **Find that last feedback source.** Ask parents or peers to read through your second-to-last draft.
   - Ask them to indicate areas that still might need attention.
   - Remember not to take their constructive suggestions as negative criticism. Be happy they're willing to help, and be sure to express your gratitude.

4. **Make those last revisions last.** Integrate any changes, and write your FINAL draft on the next seven pages.

Lunchbox
Lessons
LLC

_____

_____

_____

_____

_____

_____

_____

_____

_____

_____

_____

_____

_____

_____

_____

_____

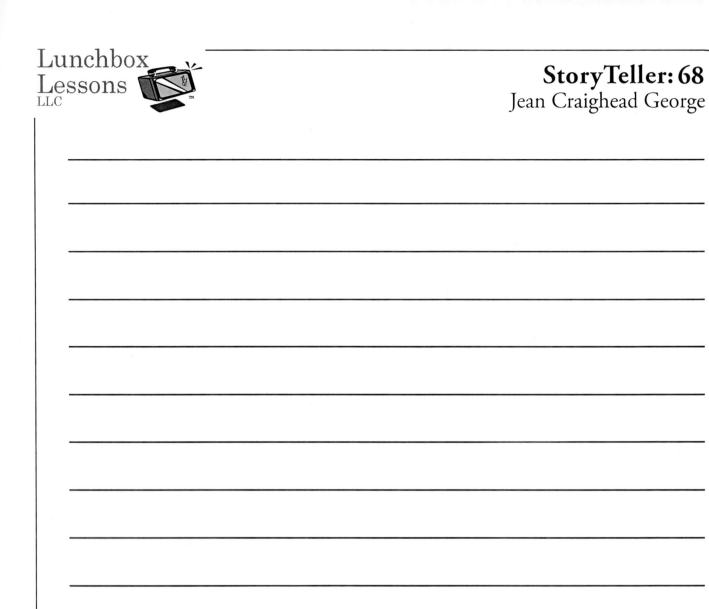

_____

_____

_____

_____

_____

_____

_____

_____

_____

_____

_____

_____

_____

_____

Lunchbox Lessons LLC

Activity Extension

Read your story aloud to a younger audience — a sibling or a friend's younger brother or sister, for example. Be dramatic as you read, and use different voices for your characters. You could even use props!

Activity 11: *Calling all Editors*

Media Connection

Watch the documentary *StoryTeller: Jean Craighead George*, which can be found at a retailer near you.

Use the Internet to search for publication opportunities.

Activity Map

1. **Reaching a wider audience.** Young authors have many opportunities available to them for sharing what it is they have written. In addition to sharing stories with family and friends, they can submit their writing to publishers and enter writing contests.

2. **Think of family and friends.** Family and friends are the first publishing scenario to explore. Make copies of your story, complete with illustrations, and give these hardcopies of your work as gifts to friends and family. Don't just think of those really close to you; think of friends who have moved away or family members you don't see often. List such possible recipients below.

_____

_____

_____

_____

_____

_____

_____

3. **Think locally.** Ask yourself if there are local publishing possibilities. Does a local newspaper, magazine, school publication or religious or club newsletter come to mind? List such possible local publishing opportunities on the lines below.

_____

_____

_____

_____

_____

4. **Think bigger.** There are many national and state-wide writing competitions for young authors. List some of these competitions below, then circle a few that you think you could submit your story to.

_____

_____

_____

_____

_____

5. **Find an agent.** There are literary agents who are specifically interested in young writers. One source of these agents is *The Agents Directory*, by Rachel Vater. Find other publishing house or agent directory resources by searching on the Internet and visiting your local library. List those additional sources on the lines below.

_____

_____

_____

_____

6. **Make your choice!** Decide which publication venue is best for you, following the advice below.
   - Don't try to tackle all publication opportunities at one time.
   - Follow directions exactly. Editors and writing contest judges always outline requirements for submission. Be careful to follow all the details so your story is recieved well. Be patient. Often a lot of time passes before you hear the results of a writing competition or the response from a publisher or agent.
   - Don't be discouraged by rejection or critical comments. Most famous authors received many rejections before they published their first work.

Thank You Wendell Minor

For your fine artwork and support of the
Lunchbox Lessons StoryTeller: Jean Craighead George series.

More Jean Craighead George books
with cover illustrations by Wendell Minor

Lunchbox Lessons LLC

Educational materials for a new world

Now is an especially exciting time for teachers, parents and students of all ages. With exciting multimedia tools and boundless information at our fingertips, education has renewed possibilities. At Lunchbox Lessons we have realized these possibilities by developing educational materials with high entertainment value that truly engage students, making the entire world around them a classroom. But compelling students to investigate, reason and create is just part of the fun; our flexible curriculums also give creativity back to learners with innovative lesson plans and workbooks that encourage imagination and explore knowledge through a world of angles — from print to DVD, audio to visual, scholastic to practical and art to science.

Inspiring tools for the modern day classroom and beyond

Pioneering new ways of learning is what Lunchbox Lessons does best, and award-winning educators and field experts are at the forefront of our efforts. By inviting learners of all kinds to take curiosity to the next level — from the bookshelves to the web to the great outdoors — we make education a treasure to be unearthed and the world a web of connections to be discovered, connections which then forge new channels for information and ideas. Exhibiting projects, collaborating with others and harnessing the powers of technology are all just part of the Lunchbox Lessons educational experience.

See it. Hear it. Know it. Use it.

Our one-stop online resource room just keeps growing, and you'll find our energy and expertise know no bounds. Each Lunchbox Lessons' series may include any of a variety of elements: WorkBooks; LessonPlans; literature; DVDs; BrainSnacks; interviews with authors, scientists and artists; and plenty of other ways to touch the senses.

Be sure to check out these exciting Lunchbox Lessons Series

StoryTellers Series bridges fact and fantasy with:

Jean Craighead George

Ken Thomasma

T.A. Barron

First Breath Series goes deep with:

Gray Whales

Harbor Seals

Killer Whales

Manatees

Sea Otters

Spotted Dolphins

The whole environment is in your backyard with:

Backyard Pioneers

Chasing El Nino

Cougar At Our Door

EarthFire

Southern Oceans

What's Up in the Universe

Printed in the United States
153039LV00001B/25/P